Chinese

IMMIGRATION AND THE AMERICAN WAY OF LIFE

Geologically speaking, the continent of North America is very old. The people who live here, by comparison, are new arrivals. Even the first settlers, the American Indians who came here from Asia about 35,000 years ago, are fairly new, not to speak of the first European settlers who came by ship or the refugees who flew in yesterday. Whenever they came, they were all immigrants. How all these immigrants live together today to form one society has been compared to the making of a mosaic. A mosaic is a picture formed from many different pieces. Thus, in America many groups of people—from African Americans or Albanians to Tibetans or Welsh—live side by side. This human mosaic was put together by the immigrants themselves, with courage, hard work, and luck. Each group of immigrants has its own history and own reasons for coming to America. Immigrants from different regions have their own way of creating communities for themselves and their children. In creating those communities, they not only keep elements of their own heritage alive, but also enrich further the fabric of American society. Each book in *Recent American Immigrants* will examine a part of this human mosaic up close. The books will look at some of the most recent arrivals to find out what they are like and how they fit into the whole mosaic.

Recent American Immigrants

CHINESE

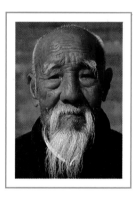

Jodine
Mayberry

Consultant
Roger Daniels, Department of History
University of Cincinnati

Franklin Watts

New York • London • Toronto • Sydney

Developed by: 𝛺 **Visual Education Corporation**
Princeton, NJ

Maps: Patricia R. Isaacs/Parrot Graphics

Cover photograph: © Alon Reininger/Contact Stock

Library of Congress Cataloging-in-Publication Data

Mayberry, Jodine
Chinese/Jodine Mayberry
p.   cm. — (Recent American Immigrants)
Includes bibliographical references
Summary: Discusses Chinese immigrants to America, their reasons for
coming, their lifestyles, and their contributions to their new country.
ISBN 0-531-10977-1
1. Chinese Americans — Juvenile literature. 2. United States — Emigration
and immigration — Juvenile literature. 3. China — Emigration and
immigration — Juvenile literature. [1. Chinese Americans.] I. Title.
II. Series: Recent American immigrants.
E184.C5G67 1990
973'.04951 — dc20   90-12273 CIP AC

Contents

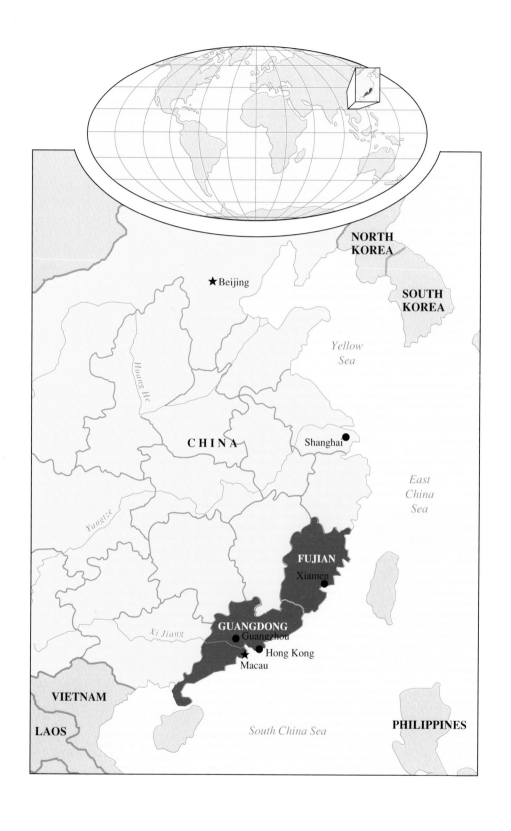

NORTH KOREA

SOUTH KOREA

★ Beijing

Yellow Sea

C H I N A

Huang He

Shanghai ●

East China Sea

Yangtze

FUJIAN

Xiamen ●

Xi Jiang

GUANGDONG

Guangzhou ●

● Hong Kong

★ Macau

VIETNAM

LAOS

South China Sea

PHILIPPINES

Era of the Laborers, 1849–1882

Few Chinese lived in America before 1850. Most Chinese immigrated following the discovery of gold in California in 1848. Many Chinese immigrants came to California in hopes of striking it rich. Then they planned to return to their families as wealthy people. Many people came from other countries with the same idea.

Some did return home, but thousands of others stayed to help build America. The Chinese were the earliest of the recent immigrants. They have a longer history here than most other immigrant groups.

Chinese Americans differed from most other Americans in their looks, language, and customs. As a result, they suffered a great deal of prejudice and violence. But they had the courage and patience to overcome these ordeals and become a proud part of the American mosaic.

ORIGINS OF THE CHINESE IMMIGRANTS

The Chinese who came to America came almost entirely from two provinces, Guangdong and Fujian in southeastern China. Many of the people in these two provinces were opposed to the Manchu dynasty, the rulers of China. They staged several unsuccessful rebellions against the Manchu rulers.

For centuries, most of China was closed to foreigners. The Chinese people had little knowledge of the outside world. Starting in 1842, though, foreign merchants gained more access to China. People in Guangdong and Fujian were able to meet them and learn about America. The people in those provinces then traveled to nearby Hong Kong or Macao, the main ports for ships crossing the Pacific. From there, they could book inexpensive passage to America, sometimes on credit.

WHY THEY CAME

People in the port cities heard that gold had been found in California from foreign sailors and merchants. Like most other people in China, they were very poor. Many of them had also been victims of the rebellions and wars. The Chinese heard many stories about the easy riches to be had in America. It is said that some European immigrants believed the streets of America were paved with gold. Some Chinese may have had a similar idea. After all, the Chinese characters that named California could be translated as "Golden Mountain."

THE GOLD RUSH

One rainy day in January of 1848, James Marshall was surveying a California stream where he was going to build a sawmill for his employer, John Sutter, a recent immigrant from Switzerland. As he examined the stream, he spotted several small bits of yellow metal gleaming in the water. Marshall had found gold.

Within a year, perhaps 150,000 people came to California from all over the world. The great gold rush of 1849 was on. The promise of quick wealth attracted 50,000 Chinese immigrants over the next ten years. Nearly all of them went to California.

The first Chinese immigrants came to California to seek their fortunes during the Gold Rush.

SOJOURNERS

Ninety percent of the Chinese who came to the United States in the nineteenth century were adult males. They called themselves by the Chinese word for sojourners. A sojourner is a person who stays in a place for a limited time. Other immigrant groups also included sojourners. Some of these intended sojourners actually stayed in America. But large numbers of immigrants, including many Chinese, actually did return to their homeland.

LIFE IN CALIFORNIA

How curious the first Chinese immigrants and the people of California must have seemed to each other! Each group was surprised at people who looked and dressed so differently and who spoke such a strange, odd-sounding language.

Nearly all the Chinese immigrants who came to America arrived at San Francisco. It became the hub of their life in America. They called it *dai fou,* or "big city." Some stayed in San Francisco. They lived together in cheap, crowded tenements in one poor area of the city. That area quickly became known as "Chinatown."

However, most of the earliest immigrants lived in rural areas. Many headed for the gold fields to pan for gold. Others became farmers and raised crops to feed the residents of California.

Chinese farmers raised fruit and vegetables all over California. Here, they are tending an orange grove.

BUILDERS OF AMERICA

Mining   The Chinese immigrants were very good miners. They went to work in gold, silver, copper, and coal mines all over the West. They established new Chinatowns in many mining towns like Butte, Montana; Denver, Colorado; and Rock Springs, Wyoming.

Farming   Many Chinese had been farmers in China, and they continued to farm in the United States. They bought small farms or leased farms from white owners. They raised fruits and vegetables all over the state, from San Francisco to San Diego.

Railroads   The Chinese are well known for their work building the western part of the first transcontinental railroad. The railroad stretched from the Atlantic to the Pacific oceans. The Chinese were hired because they were reliable, hard-working laborers. About 10,000 Chinese worked on the railroad. They earned $35 a month, which was good pay then.

Entrepreneurs   Many Chinese became entrepreneurs, people who start businesses. They ran laundries, boarding houses, and restaurants for the miners and for other Chinese. Some were merchants who imported goods from China to sell in the United States.

The number of Chinese in the United States grew as more immigrants came to provide this labor. The vast majority of these Chinese lived in the West. In 1880, more than 95 percent lived in western states.

CHINESE POPULATION IN THE UNITED STATES	
1870	60,000
1882	125,000

"CHINESE MUST GO"

In 1869, when the railroad was finished, all of the Chinese laborers were laid off. At that time, the economy of California was going through a bad period. Many people did not have jobs. Labor leaders and others felt that Chinese Americans had taken jobs that should have been held by whites. In addition, many other Americans were very prejudiced against Chinese Americans. Here are two verses from a popular song published in 1877. It was sung to the tune of *The Wearin' o' the Green*.

Twelve Hundred More

O workingmen dear, and did you hear
The news that's goin' round?
Another China steamer
Has been landed here in town.
Today I read the papers,
And it grieved my heart full sore
To see upon the title page,
O, just "Twelve Hundred More!"

O, California's coming down,
As you can plainly see.
They are hiring all the Chinamen
And discharging you and me;
But strife will be in every town
Throughout the Pacific shore,
And the cry of old and young shall be,
"O, damn, 'Twelve Hundred More.'"

Source: As quoted in Linda Perrin, *Coming to America: Immigrants from the Far East* (New York: Delacorte, 1980), pp. 32–33.

This combination of prejudice and high unemployment caused white people to mistreat the Chinese. In many places, they were beaten in the streets, and their homes and businesses were destroyed.

In the mining towns, Chinese miners were the victims of great violence. A mob destroyed Denver's Chinatown and hanged a Chinese laundryman in 1880. In Rock Springs, Wyoming, white miners killed 28 Chinese workers in 1885. Two years later in Hell's Canyon, Oregon, a white gang murdered 31 Chinese miners. No one was ever punished for any of these crimes.

The Kearney Manifesto   Between 1870 and 1882, many white Americans tried to drive out the Chinese Americans and shut the door to any further immigration. Dennis Kearney, himself a recent immigrant from Ireland, founded the Workingmen's Party. This was a political group that wanted to attract the votes of working people. Its top demand was that "the Chinese must go."

In 1877, the Workingmen's Party issued a manifesto, or statement, that said:

> *Before the world we declare that the Chinaman must leave our shores. We declare that white men, women, and boys and girls cannot live as the people of the great republic should live and compete with the single Chinese [worker] in the labor market. We declare that we cannot hope to drive the Chinaman away by working cheaper than he does. None but an enemy would expect it of us; none but an idiot could hope for success; none but a degraded coward and slave would make the effort. Death is preferable to life on a par with the Chinaman.*

The California Constitution   California adopted a new state constitution in 1879. The Workingmen's Party succeeded in inserting several anti-Chinese sections into the new constitution. It said that companies and local governments could not hire Chinese workers. The new constitution also enabled towns and cities to pass laws that would keep Chinese residents living in isolated neighborhoods.

THE CHINESE EXCLUSION ACT

From 1870 onward, agitators in California and all over the United States sought laws to prevent more Chinese laborers from coming to America. Business owners liked to hire Chinese workers because they were quick to learn. They worked for lower wages than whites and they did not go on strike often. But white workers resented this competition.

There was a racial element to anti-Chinese feeling as well. Whites' dislike of Chinese laborers was made stronger by mistrust of Chinese because they were Oriental. Many white people of the time believed that whites were superior to Orientals.

In addition, some people called Chinese Americans heathen savages because most followed a non-Christian religion. For some, Chinese Americans were heathens even if they had converted to Christianity. They were also supposed to be dirty and live in filthy slums, a charge leveled against dozens of immigrant and ethnic groups at one time or another.

The California legislature and the city of San Francisco passed several laws against the Chinese. One law, the Cubic Air ordinance, even limited housing space by restricting how much air homes should have. Most of the laws were struck down by the courts. More and more white people began to look to Congress for help since only Congress had the power to make laws about immigration.

Finally, in 1882, the U.S. Congress passed the Chinese Exclusion Act. This law barred the immigration of Chinese laborers for ten years. It continued to permit Chinese merchants and students to immigrate. The law was extended for ten years in 1892 and made permanent in 1902. At that time there were about 125,000 Chinese in the United States, which had a population of more than 50 million people. So about one person in 500 was Chinese.

Yung Wing

Not all Chinese came to America to work. Some came to study in American schools. Yung Wing was one of America's most prominent Chinese immigrants. He was born in China in 1828. When he was nineteen, he came to America to study. In 1850, he entered Yale University. Four years later, Yung Wing became the first Chinese student to graduate from an American university.

After his graduation, he became a businessman. He also served as a representative of the Chinese government to the United States. One of his jobs was to help other Chinese students come to the United States to study.

While he was at Yale, Yung Wing had become a Christian and a naturalized American citizen. He married a white American, Mary L. Kellogg, in 1875. In 1898 Yung Wing took a trip to China. When he wanted to return to the United States, he was told that his naturalization was now considered illegal. The government revoked his citizenship. Yung Wing remained in China until 1902 and then returned to the United States illegally. He lived in Connecticut until his death in 1912.

More about Yung Wing is found in his autobiography, *My Life in China and America.*

Era of Exclusion, 1882–1943

The Exclusion Act of 1882 brought about several changes for Chinese Americans in the United States. No more laborers could come to work in the mines and factories. Newcomers had to go to great lengths to prove that they were merchants or students. Some immigrants entered the country using false papers. The Chinese could no longer travel freely back and forth from the United States to their homeland. Like Yung Wing, they were not allowed to return to the United States if they were not merchants or students or might not satisfy new citizenship requirements.

Most Chinese immigrants moved from rural areas to big cities. Many took service jobs, such as waiting on tables in restaurants. Many Chinese drifted into jobs known at the time as "women's work." They cooked, washed clothes, or became household servants.

Chinese Americans formed groups or associations. Many of these groups became national organizations, such as the Chinese Consolidated Benevolent Association (known as the Six Companies). These organizations helped poor immigrants and kept order among the Chinese. They helped the Chinese survive in America.

THE POPULATION DECLINES

Under the Exclusion Act, Chinese laborers could not bring their wives to America from China. Only merchants could bring their wives over. In addition, there were very few Chinese women already living in the United States for single men to marry. According to the 1880 census, 105,465 Chinese lived in America, but only 4,779 of them were women. That meant there were twenty-one men for every woman. By 1890, the ratio was even worse—twenty-seven men for every woman.

Chinese laborers who were citizens could bring their children to America. Chinese immigrants could not become naturalized citizens after living in the country for a certain number of years, but children born in the United States became citizens automatically. When they became adults, these Chinese with American citizenship often went to China to get married. They could bring their children to America, but not their wives, the children's mothers. Those who brought children over usually brought sons, not daughters. As a result, from 1906 to 1924, only about 150 Chinese women a year entered the United States.

All of these factors combined to prevent Chinese immigrants from forming families and increasing their numbers. This fact, combined with the barring of immigration to China, reduced the number of Chinese in the United States. In fact, the Chinese American population declined steadily until the 1920s.

CHINESE IN THE UNITED STATES

1880	105,465
1920	61,639

Source: U.S. Census.

IMMIGRATION PROCEDURES

After the 1882 Exclusion Act, newly arriving Chinese immigrants had to prove that they were merchants, students, or travelers, not laborers. Each immigrant had to have at least two non-Chinese Americans vouch for him or her.

Legal Chinese immigrants had to carry residence certificates. If they were arrested without their certificates, they could be deported. Some immigrants bought false certificates so they could bring relatives to the United States.

From 1882 to 1940, Chinese Americans continued to move to big cities and to the Midwest and East Coast. While San Francisco remained *dai fou,* by 1940, New York, Los Angeles, Oakland, Chicago, Seattle, Portland, Sacramento, and Boston all had large Chinese communities. San Francisco was still the most significant community. Almost 20 percent of all Chinese in America lived in that city.

CHINESE POPULATION IN CITIES, 1940

San Francisco	17,782
New York	12,302
Los Angeles	5,000 (approx.)
Oakland	3,201

Source: Roger Daniels, *Asian America* (Seattle: University of Washington Press, 1988), pp. 69–70.

Chicago, Seattle, and Portland, Oregon, each had approximately 2,000 Chinese, and Sacramento and Boston each had between 1,000 and 2,000 Chinese.

As these cities came to have larger Chinese communities, the number of Chinese in smaller towns went down. Butte, Montana, went from 710 Chinese in 1890 to 88 in 1940.

THE SHED AND ANGEL ISLAND

From 1882 to 1910, Chinese immigrants arriving in San Francisco were held in a kind of jail on the waterfront called "the shed." It was here that merchants and students waited while government agents processed their papers. They had to pay their own expenses while they were locked up.

After 1910, Asian immigrants were held on Angel Island in San Francisco Bay. Some people have said that Angel Island was similar to Ellis Island in New York harbor, but there was a difference. European immigrants arrived at Ellis Island where they received brief physical examinations. Those who passed (about 98 percent) were allowed to enter the United States. Those who failed were sent back. Ellis Island was a way station where immigrants stopped briefly. Angel Island was different. Both were called islands of hope and tears, but at Ellis Island it was mostly hope—and at Angel Island it was mostly tears.

Asian immigrants, like this group arriving in about 1911, came to San Francisco's Angel Island.

The 1906 San Francisco earthquake destroyed City Hall (shown here), including the records of many Chinese.

THE 1906 EARTHQUAKE

The great San Francisco earthquake of 1906 created an opportunity for many Chinese. The earthquake and fires destroyed much of the city. They also destroyed most of the city's immigration records. As a result, many Chinese were able to get new documents saying they were born in the United States. The fake papers allowed them to return to China and bring back sons. The people they brought back were often not their sons. They might be children of relatives or friends. They were called "paper sons" in Chinatown.

When they arrived, the paper sons were held at Angel Island. There, government officials questioned them repeatedly. The officials hoped to catch them in a lie so they could be sent back to China. Agents would ask them questions like, "How many steps in your house?" or "Do you have a dog?" Many paper sons outwitted the agents. To answer the questions, they memorized information about their false families from crib sheets.

Between 1883 and 1943, 95,000 people immigrated from China. That equaled about 1,500 immigrants a year.

During those years, the overwhelming majority of immigrants continued to be adult men. They created bachelor societies in each Chinatown. They lived together in boarding houses. After work, the men liked to gamble for recreation. They played card games like faro and poker.

Although more and more families with children were living in American Chinatowns, most of the immigrants' families remained back home in China. One writer has called these families "mutilated families" because husbands and wives lived apart for so many years. Mutilated families outnumbered united families among Chinese Americans until after World War II.

Here is part of a letter that a mother in China wrote to a relative in the United States about her son:

> *I hear that my son is playing the prodigal, being idle, or spending his earnings for unnecessary articles of clothing. . . . I authorize you, his near relative and senior in years, to strenuously admonish him. If moderate chastisement fails, then call to your aid one or more of your brothers (relatives) and sorely beat him, not pitying his body.*
>
> Source: As quoted in Ronald Takaki, *Strangers from Another Shore* (Boston: Little, Brown, 1989), p. 129.

CHINESE SOCIETY

In most places, Chinese Americans were forced to live in their own communities. But the Chinatowns were also places where they could live freely among friends. They could speak their own language, eat familiar food, and do the same things they did back home in China. The merchants became the leaders of the Chinese American community. A large number of Chinese worked in stores and restaurants in Chinatowns. Many also took manufacturing jobs. They worked in factories that made clothing, cigars, and shoes.

The Chinese formed associations based on their family or clan names. People who shared the same name, such as Wong, joined together as if they were related. The associations provided help for poor widows and orphans. Family associations also acted as law courts to settle disputes among members. Arguments between different families might be settled by the Six Companies.

Here is a glimpse into what the life of a merchant's wife was like from a woman who lived in Butte's Chinatown. In the beginning, her life in America seems to have been even more restricted than it had been in China:

> *When I came to America as a bride, I never knew I would be coming to a prison. Until the [1911] Revolution [in China], I was allowed out of the house but once a year. That was during New Years when families exchanged . . . calls and feasts.*
>
> *The women were always glad to see each other; we exchanged news of our families and friends in China. We admired each other's clothes and jewels. We ate separately from the men . . . . Sometimes we went to a feast when a baby born into a family association was a month old. Otherwise we seldom visited each other; it was considered immodest to be seen too many times during the year.*
>
> *After the Revolution in China, I heard that women there were free to go out. When the father of my children cut his queue he adopted new habits; I discarded my Chinese clothes and began to wear American clothes. By that time my children were going to American schools, could speak English, and they helped me buy what I needed. Gradually the other women followed my example. We began to go out more frequently and since then I go out all the time.*
>
> Source: As quoted in Roger Daniels, *Asian America* (Seattle: University of Washington Press, 1988), pp. 82–83.

Until the 1940s, America's Chinatowns were isolated homes
for most Chinese Americans. After World War II, they became
tourist attractions. This photograph shows how San
Francisco's Chinatown looked in 1945.

OUTSIDERS

Chinese Americans were very isolated from other Americans in their Chinatowns. They felt like outsiders, as though they had not become part of America. Some immigrants lived most of their lives in Chinatown without ever learning more than a few words of English. Children in San Francisco and other places went to segregated schools.

When the first American-born Chinese children started attending American schools, other children teased them and called them names. Their parents would tell them to ignore the names and work hard in school to get ahead.

But even with good American educations, many Chinese American young people had great difficulty finding jobs outside of Chinatown. Prejudice forced Chinese into low-paying manual labor. The parents of these American-educated children found that their dreams for their children's success were not being fulfilled. Thus, many parents urged their sons to go back to China, where their skills and training could be put to work. Chinese American author Jade Snow Wong has written how her older brother, an American-born graduate of an American university, planned to return to China to get his medical degree:

> *Father and son agreed that the study of medicine in China would prepare Older Brother for his career. Knowing the Chinese language, he could establish himself where medical personnel was greatly needed, and he could strengthen his ancestral ties by visits to Daddy's native village and relatives.*
> —Jade Snow Wong,
> *Fifth Chinese Daughter*

Era of Limited Immigration, 1947-1965

In the 1930s, moviemakers in Hollywood released several movies about a Chinese detective named Charlie Chan (always played by a white actor) from books written by Earl Derr Biggers. In these books and movies Chan was portrayed as being very wise and mysterious and as having many children. His American-born and educated sons were painted as being shallow and carefree. These images are stereotypes, or set ideas about the way a group of people acts or looks. They are too simple. Most Chinese Americans were not like Chan or his sons.

Also in the 1930s, Pearl S. Buck began writing novels about China. She was the daughter of a missionary sent to China to do religious and educational work there. She lived in China for several years. In 1931 the Japanese army invaded China. She wrote about the bravery and suffering of the Chinese people during the war and under Japanese occupation. Her novel *The Good Earth* told the story of a Chinese peasant family struggling to survive war and poverty. Pearl Buck's books and the movies made from them helped millions of Americans learn about China and the Chinese people.

Americans were impressed by the way the Chinese resisted the Japanese. Then the Japanese attacked the United States by bombing Pearl Harbor in 1941. The United States entered the war, and the United States and China became allies. The war by then had become a worldwide conflict.

World War II was an important turning point for Chinese Americans. During the war, Americans continued to gain respect for the Chinese. They saw the Chinese people fighting valiantly to expel the Japanese from their country. Chiang Kai-shek, the leader of the Chinese army, became a popular figure in the United States.

Chinese soldiers, like these in Shanghai, stalled invading Japanese troops in 1937 with rifles and hand grenades.

The leader of China, Chiang Kai-shek, seemed a heroic figure on both sides of the Pacific during World War II.

This aided in changing people's minds about allowing more Chinese to immigrate. In 1943 a group of well-known Americans formed a committee to repeal the exclusion law. They wanted to allow Chinese to enter the country under the quota system, just as other immigrants did. In this system, a certain number of immigrants were allowed from each country each year. The committee quickly succeeded in convincing Congress to repeal the exclusion law. Even under the quota system, only 105 Chinese were allowed to come to the United States each year. However, now Chinese Americans were able to become naturalized citizens.

After the war, the government allowed many more Chinese to enter the United States. Some were refugees left homeless by the war. Others were wives and relatives of Chinese Americans who had fought in the war.

CHINESE AMERICANS IN THE 1940s

In 1940, 77,504 Chinese lived in the United States, down from a peak of about 125,000 in 1882. A very large number of these people were still adult males with wives back in China. By 1950, the Chinese American population rose to about 117,000 people—76,725 men and 40,415 women.

THE WOMEN ARRIVE

The greatest change among Chinese Americans in the 1940s was the arrival of large numbers of Chinese women. The immigrants' wives were finally allowed to join them. In addition, many Chinese Americans who had served in the armed forces during World War II married women in China. In eight years, from 1945 to 1952, nearly 10,000 women came to America. During the 1940s, Chinese Americans had an estimated 20,000 children.

CHINESE IN THE UNITED STATES 1880–1950

1880	105,465
1890	107,620
1900	89,863
1910	71,531
1920	61,639
1930	74,954
1940	77,504
1950	117,140

Source: U.S. Census.

The brave service of Chinese American soldiers helped change white Americans' attitudes toward all Chinese Americans.

CHANGING ATTITUDES

About 16,000 Chinese Americans served in the armed forces during World War II. This was a very large number—about one in five of all Chinese Americans. These soldiers and sailors fought well for their country. Most of the American public approved of the repeal of the Exclusion Act, and because of the war, people learned even more about China and about Chinese Americans. Chinatowns became tourist attractions. People would go there to see the sights, eat Chinese food, and buy goods imported from China.

Chinese Americans began to enter the mainstream of American life. Those with educations were able to get good jobs outside of Chinatown. Other Americans began to realize that Chinese Americans were Americans too.

The United States also feared the spread of communism in Korea, a large Asian country on a peninsula south of China. After the war, Korea was split into Communist North Korea and non-Communist South Korea. In 1950, North Korea invaded South Korea. The United Nations (UN) sent millions of troops to South Korea to help it fight the Communists. Aside from Koreans, most of the troops were Americans and British, but soldiers from Australia, Greece, Canada, and many other countries also fought in the Korean War on the side of the UN forces. (The map on the next page shows the location of North and South Korea.)

Communist China was an ally of North Korea. It sent millions of troops to help North Korea fight the United Nations forces. After three years of fighting, the Korean War ended in 1953 with an armistice, when both sides agreed to stop fighting. North and South Korea remained two separate countries, one Communist and one not. Hostility between the two countries remains, and American troops are still stationed in South Korea.

A COMMUNITY DIVIDED

The war in Korea, which cost the lives of many Americans, intensified anti-Communist feelings at home. Strong laws against Communist activity were passed. Some people who were suspected of being Communists were questioned by the government and lost their jobs. It was a time of fear and upset, and some people were treated unfairly.

All of this put the Chinese American community in a difficult position. By 1950, nearly half of all Chinese Americans had been born in the United States. Most Chinese had become citizens and thought of themselves as Americans. Nevertheless, they still tried to keep close ties with friends and family in China.

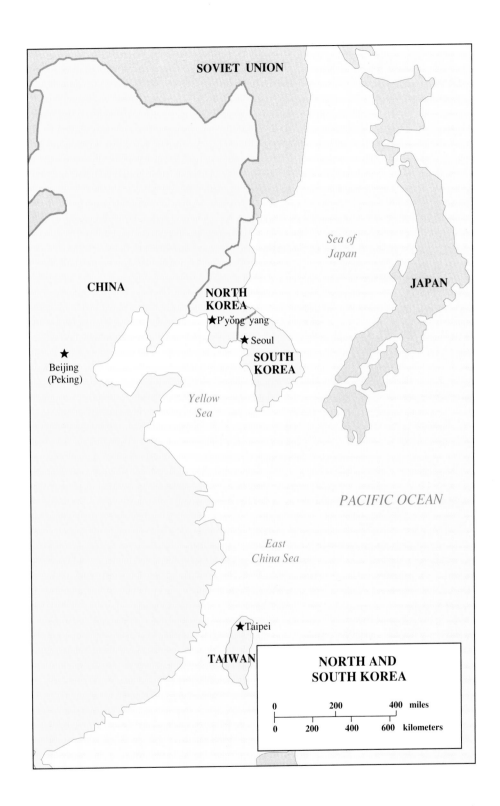

SOVIET UNION

CHINA

NORTH
KOREA
★P'yŏng yang
★ Seoul
SOUTH
KOREA

★
Beijing
(Peking)

Sea of
Japan

JAPAN

Yellow
Sea

PACIFIC OCEAN

East
China Sea

★Taipei

TAIWAN

NORTH AND
SOUTH KOREA

0	200	400	miles
0	200	400	600	kilometers

35

Just as the war divided the people in China, it split the Chinese American community. Most had supported Chiang Kai-shek, but a few had favored Mao. In addition, Chinese Americans found themselves cut off from their homeland. Some could not contact their relatives in Communist China for many years.

REFUGEES FROM CHINA

Wars and natural disasters often leave people without homes or the means to earn a living. These people are called refugees. The wars in China and Korea left thousands of refugees. Starting in 1948, Congress passed laws allowing hundreds of thousands of refugees from Europe to settle in the United States. In 1950, Congress passed a law to help some refugees from Asia to settle in the United States as well. The law permitted 4,000 European refugees who had been living in China for many years to enter the country. These were mainly people who, from 1917 to the early 1940s, had fled from Soviet Russia or from Nazi Germany.

Three years later, in 1953, Congress changed the law to allow 2,000 refugees from China to enter the United States. The refugees had to be approved by the government in Taiwan. This marked the first time that America had ever admitted Asian refugees. It was an important first step. Later, in the 1970s and 1980s, this small trickle would grow into a flood as hundreds of thousands of Vietnamese, Kampucheans, and other Asians came to America following the Vietnam War.

STRANDED STUDENTS

One result of the Communist takeover of China was that it left about 5,000 Chinese students stranded in the United States. Most of the students had won scholarships from the Chinese

36

government to study in the United States. They were China's best students. The U.S. government gave them the choice of staying in America or going back to China. Most of the students chose to stay. As teachers and scientists, they contributed a great deal to the growth of post-war America.

RED HUNTING

During the 1950s, government agencies such as the Federal Bureau of Investigation searched for Communists among American citizens and immigrants. These "red hunters" suspected that some Chinese Americans were Communists because of their ties to people back in China. This scared people in the Chinese American community. They were afraid that if they were labeled as Communists, they would be sent back to Red China.

In 1950, the government passed the Emergency Detention Act. This law allowed the government to arrest and imprison people they suspected of being Communist spies. During World War II, the government had imprisoned 120,000 Japanese Americans in camps enclosed in barbed wire. This was intended to prevent them from spying or working for the Japanese government. Chinese Americans feared the new law would be used to do the same thing to them. Fortunately the law was never used against any Chinese immigrants.

HAWAIIAN STATEHOOD

Hawaii became the fiftieth state in 1959. It was an important event for both Chinese Americans and Japanese Americans. It had taken Hawaiians a long time to win statehood. One reason was racism. Most of the people in Hawaii were of Asian origin. The majority were of Japanese, Chinese, or Filipino origin, although most had been born on American soil. Thus, 90 percent of them were American citizens. Some U.S. senators, particularly those from the South, opposed statehood for Hawaii, but most people favored it. In the very first congressional election after statehood, the people of Hawaii elected a Chinese American to the U.S. Senate and a Japanese American to the House of Representatives.

Hiram Fong

The first Asian American to be elected to the U.S. Senate was Hiram Leong Fong of Hawaii. He was born in Honolulu in 1907. His parents came to Hawaii from Guangdong province in China in 1872 to work on a sugar plantation. Fong was the seventh of eleven children. He went to work at an early age shining shoes and selling newspapers.

Fong graduated from the University of Hawaii and Harvard Law School. Then he joined a law firm made up of Chinese, Japanese, Korean, and white attorneys. Fong became a millionaire by investing in real estate. A Republican, he served many years in Hawaii's territorial legislature. Fong served in the U.S. Senate until 1977.

CHINESE AMERICA IN 1960

By 1960, Chinese Americans had become well established in this country. Three-fifths of them lived in four western states: California, Hawaii, Oregon, and Washington.

By 1960, more than 60 percent of the Chinese American population had been born in the United States. Many took American first names. Often they also changed the spellings of their last names so they were easier for non-Chinese to pronounce. These native-born citizens dressed in American-style clothes and spoke unaccented English.

Though they were generally well educated, Chinese Americans earned less than whites. Discrimination kept almost half in low-paying jobs (see the chart). Nevertheless, the Chinese were becoming middle-class Americans and beginning to enjoy prosperity in their adopted land.

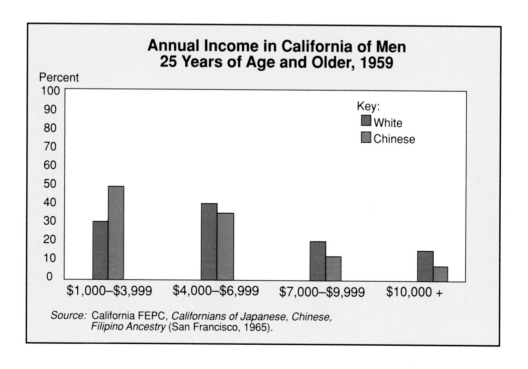

Annual Income in California of Men 25 Years of Age and Older, 1959

Key:
White
Chinese

Source: California FEPC, *Californians of Japanese, Chinese, Filipino Ancestry* (San Francisco, 1965).

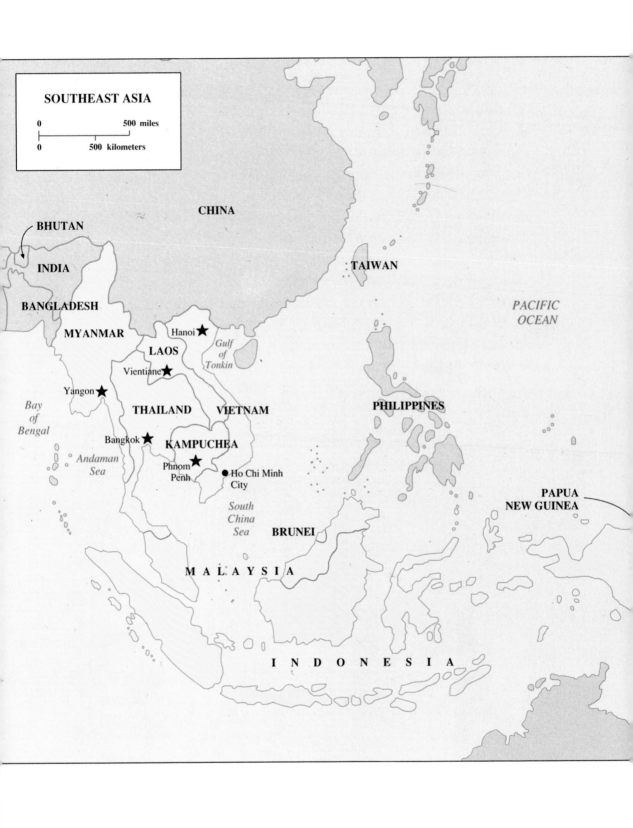

SOUTHEAST ASIA

0   500   miles

0   500   kilometers

CHINA

BHUTAN

INDIA

BANGLADESH

TAIWAN

MYANMAR

Hanoi ★

Gulf of Tonkin

LAOS

Vientiane ★

Yangon ★

Bay of Bengal

THAILAND

VIETNAM

PACIFIC OCEAN

PHILIPPINES

Andaman Sea

Bangkok ★

KAMPUCHEA

Phnom Penh ★

● Ho Chi Minh City

South China Sea

BRUNEI

M A L A Y S I A

PAPUA NEW GUINEA

I N D O N E S I A

Era of the Asian Refugees, 1965 to the Present

Throughout American history, most of the country's immigrants have come from Europe. At first they came from northern Europe—from England, Ireland, Scotland, and Scandinavia. Later they came from southern Europe—from Italy, Greece, and Portugal.

In the 1960s, the pattern of immigration changed dramatically. From 1965 onward, the majority of American immigrants have come from two different areas. They have come from Latin America and from Asia. There are two major reasons for the great increase in immigration from Asia: a change in immigration laws and a war.

THE IMMIGRATION ACT OF 1965

In 1965, Congress finally scrapped the old quota system that had dated from 1924. It substituted a complicated system that allowed about the same number of immigrants from both the eastern and the western hemispheres to immigrate to the United States. Total immigration has increased from about 300,000 annually in the 1960s to about 600,000 annually in the 1980s. Having a close relative in the United States was now one of the most important ways to get into the country. This made it easier for many Chinese to come here.

The Immigration Act of 1965 was much fairer to Chinese and other Asian immigrants than any earlier laws had been. It enabled a great many Chinese to come to America.

THE VIETNAM WAR

Vietnam is a large country just south of China in an area called Southeast Asia. Just like Korea, Vietnam had become divided into Communist North Vietnam and non-Communist South Vietnam. The two countries went to war with each other in the 1950s. In the early 1960s, America went to the aid of South Vietnam. The United States sent hundreds of thousands of soldiers and billions of dollars' worth of supplies to South Vietnam during the 1960s and early 1970s. Nevertheless, South Vietnam lost the war in 1975. This meant that hundreds of thousands of Vietnamese refugees would flee to America and elsewhere.

Many of these refugees are Chinese in origin. They were part of a Chinese minority in the countries they came from. In some cases, the other people in those countries suspected that they were loyal to China. Their property was taken and they were imprisoned in work camps.

After the war ended, hundreds of thousands of other Vietnamese became refugees. They boarded flimsy, leaky boats and headed for nearby countries, such as Thailand and the Philippines. These "boat people" suffered enormously. Some drowned and some were killed by pirates. Many made it to refugee camps where they had to stay for months or years. If they had friends or relatives in America who could help them, they might be allowed to come to the United States. Many did come as a result.

In the meantime, thousands of refugees came from other parts of Southeast Asia. They were also fleeing from war, Communist governments, and hunger. By 1985, there were 634,200 Vietnamese in the United States. There were also 218,400 people from Laos and 160,000 from Kampuchea. Many, of course, were born in the United States of parents who had left those lands.

GROWTH OF THE CHINESE AMERICAN POPULATION

CHINESE POPULATION IN THE UNITED STATES

1960	236,084
1970	435,062
1980	806,027
1985 (est.)	1,079,000

Source: U.S. Census.

Throughout the 1960s and 1970s, new immigrants and refugees swelled the Chinese American population.

About 103,000 people immigrated from Asia in 1971, many of them Chinese. In fact, there were so many new Chinese immigrants that the Chinese Americans began to speak of "ABCs" (American-born Chinese) and "FOBs" (fresh off the boats), to make a difference between older and newer immigrants.

By 1980, the Chinese American population had soared again to 806,027. Now, 63 percent of the Chinese in America were people who had been born in Asia, not the United States.

In the meantime, the newest immigrants were once again packed into the Chinatowns of big cities. Before 1960, New York's Chinatown had a population of less than 15,000. By 1980, it had swelled to 100,000. The new immigrants worked at low-paying jobs, such as cook, waiter, and garment worker. They struggled to learn English.

Unlike the old bachelors of the nineteenth century, the new immigrants brought their families with them.

Refugees from China were often very well educated. They were doctors and engineers and scientists.

THE COLD WAR THAWS

In the 1970s, other events besides the Vietnam War and new immigration laws helped Chinese immigrate to America. In the late 1960s and early 1970s, relations between the United States and China gradually became more friendly. Most Americans gave up on the idea that Chiang Kai-shek could ever take over Mainland China. The United States gradually stopped supporting Taiwan. In 1971, the United States joined in voting to admit China to the United Nations in place of Taiwan.

NIXON'S TRIP TO CHINA

Late in 1971, President Richard Nixon sent Henry Kissinger on a secret diplomatic mission to China. Kissinger's visit paved the way for Nixon himself to visit China for eight days in February of 1972. This marked the first time an American president had ever visited China. Nixon called his trip "a journey of peace." At the end of his visit, American and Chinese leaders issued a joint pledge to "normalize relations" between the two nations.

In 1977, Deng Xiaoping became China's leader. Deng led a movement to modernize China and open up trade with the rest of the world. Many American business owners were glad to have the chance to sell goods to the people of China.

China and the United States opened embassies in each other's countries in 1979. That same year, Deng paid a return visit to the United States. During the 1980s, China not only opened its doors to trade, it also allowed foreign tourists to visit many of its cities and historic sites. Deng sent thousands of Chinese students to the United States to study. He wanted them to get good educations so they could help modernize China. Some students liked the United States so much, they became immigrants and stayed.

What did all this mean for Chinese Americans? It meant that they were free to renew ties with old friends and family members back in China. Many even went back to China for visits. It also gave some immigrants the opportunity to start businesses selling goods imported from China.

THE MODEL MINORITY

The Asian immigrants who arrived in the 1960s and 1970s helped create a new image of the Chinese and other Asians. Americans began to notice that many of the Asian immigrants worked very hard. They learned English quickly and became naturalized citizens as soon as they could. They did not live on welfare, and they encouraged their children to do well in school.

The native-born children and grandchildren of the new immigrants have gained a reputation as a "model minority," whose members were quickly becoming members of the American middle class. The model minority was a stereotype, just as Charlie Chan had been. It was too simple to be true. It was also very unfair to other ethnic groups. Each minority group is made up of individuals. Some individuals do well, some do not. Each group has its own set of problems and prejudices to overcome.

It certainly was not true that all Asian immigrants were succeeding in America. In the 1970s, unemployment was twice as high in San Francisco's Chinatown as it was for the rest of the city. More than one-third of the residents were poor. As many as eight or ten people might live together in crowded slum apartments. Many worked in restaurants and clothing factories for low wages. The immigrants who were succeeding were the ones who arrived with good educations, good job skills, and some money in their pockets.

EXCELLING IN SCHOOL

Many Chinese immigrants have worked hard to get a good education. If they cannot go to school themselves, they work hard to provide an education for their children.

In 1970, nearly 70 percent of all Chinese Americans were high school graduates, and about one-fourth had graduated from college. Only some Japanese Americans surpass the Chinese in educational achievements.

This desire to excel in school contributes to the model minority image. Asians have an image of being smart and hardworking. It has become common now for Chinese or Vietnamese students to graduate first or second in their high school classes. Often they had come to the United States only a few years before, unable to speak English.

These images disturb some Chinese students. They feel that everyone expects them to excel in school just because they are Asians. In reality, some students are better than others, just as with any group. The students also feel that they are being pushed into the sciences when they would rather study other things. Very often, their parents insist that they major in a science, in medicine, or in mathematics. The students feel that they are being forced to fit a stereotype. They are not allowed to express their individual differences.

Halsey Junior High School in Queens, New York.

Chinese Americans are involved in all kinds of "American" activities.

MOVING TO THE SUBURBS

By 1980, many Chinese Americans had gotten college educations and found good jobs. They were finally able to move out of the Chinatowns and into the suburbs. They had reached the same point as most earlier European immigrants. They had become part of the large, fairly comfortable middle class.

These Chinese also have become very Americanized. They have moved into suburban neighborhoods and become part of the larger community. As time passed, many immigrants also turned away from some of their old Chinese customs. For example, most Chinese Americans now marry for love, just as other Americans do. They no longer allow their parents to arrange marriages for them. That was once the custom both in China and in America's Chinatowns.

DISTINGUISHED CHINESE AMERICANS

Like other immigrant groups, the Chinese have their share of distinguished members. These are people who have excelled in some way in work or study or athletics. In the next few pages, we will learn about some outstanding Chinese Americans.

I. M. Pei

Ieoh Ming Pei became interested in architecture when he was a teenager living in Shanghai, China. The city was enjoying a building boom. Everywhere Pei looked he saw cranes and scaffolds and workmen putting up tall buildings. That, he decided, was just what he wanted to do too.

Pei came to the United States in 1935 to study architecture at the University of Pennsylvania. He changed his mind, however, when he discovered he had to be able to paint pictures of the buildings he was designing. He felt he could not draw or paint well enough.

Instead Pei enrolled at the Massachusetts Institute of Technology where he studied engineering and design. He earned a bachelor's degree in architecture there in 1939. Pei had intended to return home with his new degree. However, he was stranded in the United States during World War II.

The East Building of the National Gallery of Art in Washington, D.C., designed by the Chinese American architect I. M. Pei.

During the war, he went to work as an architect in New York and Los Angeles. In 1948, Pei joined a New York firm headed by William Zeckendorf. Pei soon became an expert in designing office and apartment buildings in big cities. He also specializes now in designing low-cost apartments to house poor people cheaply. Pei wants to build attractive buildings that people would like to live in.

Pei is world famous for his beautiful buildings. He designed the John F. Kennedy Memorial Library in Boston; the American Embassy in Montevideo, Uruguay; the glass pyramid at the Louvre in Paris; and the East Building of the National Gallery in Washington, D.C.

Pei was born in Canton, China, in 1917. His father was a banker who had moved to Shanghai and to Hong Kong. Pei now lives in New York City where he heads the architectural firm of I. M. Pei and Partners.

Connie Chung

Connie Chung is probably the best-known Chinese American in the United States. She became famous as a TV news broadcaster on the NBC network. In 1989 she became the anchor on the CBS Sunday Night News, where she also filled in frequently for Dan Rather, the anchor on the CBS Evening News.

Connie Chung was born in 1946 in Washington, D.C. She was the tenth and youngest child of William Ling Chung and Margaret Chung. She was the only one of their children born in the United States. Her father had been a diplomat in Chiang Kai-shek's government. He brought his family to America in 1946. When the Communists took over China in 1949, the Chungs remained in Washington.

Connie grew up in suburban Maryland and went to college at the University of Maryland. When she graduated in 1969, she went to work for a local television station. She started out as a secretary. Then she advanced to be news writer, assignment editor, and on-the-air reporter.

In 1971, Connie Chung went to work in CBS's Washington bureau, where she covered the 1972 presidential election, the Watergate scandal, and Vice President Nelson Rockefeller.

Connie Chung went to China for the first time in 1987. While she was there, she interviewed several members of her own family about their lives in China. "I went to my grandparents' graves . . . and I cried a lot with my relatives," she later told an interviewer. "My life has been much more defined by my roots since that experience."

Tiffany Chin

When Tiffany Chin was eight years old, her mother bought her a pair of ice skates for one dollar at a garage sale. The first time Tiffany tried to use the skates, the blades bent and she sat down on the ice, hard. The skates were just toys with aluminum blades instead of steel ones.

Despite that painful beginning, Tiffany fell in love with figure skating. Within five years, she became one of the best in the world. At thirteen she won the junior world championship. In 1984, she was the youngest member of the U.S. Winter Olympic team at Sarajevo, Yugoslavia, and the next year she won the U.S. Women's Figure Skating Championship.

Tiffany Chin grew up in the Los Angeles suburb of Toluca Lake with her parents and brother and sister. Her father, a native of Oakland, California, is a scientist. Her mother immigrated from Taiwan in 1961. She is a librarian.

Tiffany Chin had to work hard to become a world-class figure skater. When she was in high school, she followed a grueling schedule. Three days a week she commuted 70 miles to an ice rink in Costa Mesa. The other four days, she practiced at a rink in North Hollywood.

At five feet one inch, Tiffany Chin is known for her small size and amazing strength. Sports writers dubbed her "China Doll," a nickname she doesn't like but has learned to live with.

Yo-Yo Ma

Yo-Yo Ma is a famous cellist who gives concerts all over the world. The "Yo" in his name means friendship. His parents, he jokes, "seem to have got lazy and been unable to think of anything else so they added another Yo."

Yo-Yo Ma's father, Hiao-Tsiun, had been a professor of music at Nanjing University in China. In 1936, he went to Paris to study music. Yo-Yo Ma's mother had been a student of his father's. Yo-Ya Ma was born in Paris in 1955. His family moved to New York in 1962. Once there, his father formed the Children's Orchestra of New York.

Yo-Yo Ma has studied music all his life. He performed in his first concert when he was five years old. He was not even as tall as the cello. When he was older, he studied music at Julliard School of Music in New York. He graduated from high school at fifteen and later from Harvard University.

Yo-Yo Ma has said that when he moved to America, "I had to deal with two . . . worlds. At home I had to submerge my identity. You can't talk back to your parents. At school, I was expected to answer back, to reveal my individuality. At home, we spoke only Chinese; we were taken to Chinese movies to remind us of our traditional values. But I was also American, growing up with American values."

Today, as a brilliant and admired performer, Yo-Yo Ma has successfully conquered both worlds. He is married to Jill Hornor, who is also a musician. They have two children.

Maya Yang Lin

Like I. M. Pei, Maya Yang Lin is an architect. Unlike Pei, she is a native-born American. Maya Lin was a twenty-one-year-old student at Yale University in 1981 when her design for the Vietnam War Memorial in Washington, D.C., was chosen over 1,420 other entries.

The memorial is a black granite, V-shaped wall inscribed with the names of the more than 50,000 Americans killed in Vietnam. The wall is set into a hillside in a park.

At first many veterans opposed Maya Lin's monument. One called it "a degrading ditch." Now it is one of the most popular tourist attractions in Washington. Millions have visited "the Wall." Everyone who sees it is moved by it.

Maya Lin grew up in a sheltered Chinese American family in Athens, Ohio. She was not prepared for the controversy the monument caused. She dropped out of college for a while, then returned and earned her degree.

In 1989, Lin was again tapped to design a memorial, this time to the American civil rights movement. She designed a granite disk, bathed in a shallow film of water. It bears the names of people who were killed fighting for civil rights. People can touch the names through the water. The memorial is located in Atlanta, Georgia.

Lin says she will not design any more memorials. "I began the decade and ended it with memorials," she says. "I feel fortunate to have done them, and I'm closing the door with a happy feeling."

CHINESE FOOD

One of the great benefits of the Chinese immigration to America is that all Americans can now enjoy Chinese cooking. In China there are four distinct *cuisines,* or styles of cooking. Each of these styles is named after the area where it was perfected.

Peking   Peking (now spelled Beijing) has long been the capital city of China. It is the city where the best chefs and restaurants can be found. Wheat is a staple in the area around the city. Noodles and breads are a major part of the cuisine. This style is famous for Peking duck, an elegantly served roast duck.

Cantonese   Cantonese is the best-known Chinese food in America. Canton is a city located in Guangdong province. Many Chinese came to America from that province, bringing their local dishes with them. Wonton soup, suckling pig, and stir-fried foods are all Cantonese dishes.

Shanghai   Shanghai is the most populous city in China. It has been a major port city for centuries. Shanghai cuisine is known for its heavy use of soy sauce, sugar, and salt-cured foods. It is also famous for its seafood dishes.

Szechuan   Szechuan (or Sichuan) cooking depends on a lot of sharp spices such as ginger, pepper, and hot chili peppers. Szechuan cooking has become popular in the United States only in the last twenty years. Hot and sour soup and Kung Boa chicken are examples of Szechuan cooking.

Ingredients   The Chinese have had 3,000 years to perfect the art of cooking. During much of that time, food has been scarce, though China is a rich country in terms of soil and climate. The Chinese treat food with great reverence. They waste virtually nothing. When they prepare a dish, they give as much thought to the color and appearance of it as to the taste.

The Chinese like to use beef, pork, chicken, duck, fish, and shellfish in their dishes. They usually chop and mix the meat with vegetables, nuts, and fruit to make it stretch further.

For spices, they use garlic, ginger, pepper, and soy sauce in many dishes. Soy sauce is used like salt to flavor most dishes. Duck sauce or plum sauce is a sweet sauce served with Peking duck and fried noodles. They use spicy sauces to enhance the flavor of bland foods like pork and chicken.

Here is a simple and delicious Chinese meal. It is easy to prepare for two or three people. However, an adult should stand by to help a young person at the stove. Read the recipes all the way through before starting to cook.

Egg Drop Soup

2 eggs, well beaten
1 Tbsp. soy sauce
1 13¾ ounce can chicken
   broth with enough
   water to make 3 cups of
   liquid altogether

1 Tbsp. minced scallion
1 Tsp. sesame or other
   cooking oil

Beat eggs. Set aside.
Pour diluted chicken broth and soy sauce into a pan.
Bring to a boil over medium high heat. Using a potholder and holding the pan carefully, stir in beaten eggs. Remove from heat to a level surface. Garnish with minced scallion and sesame oil. Use a ladle to transfer soup to bowls. Serve hot. (Always take care in handling hot liquids. They may cause bad burns if spilled.)

Beef Slices and Snow Peas

For marinating, or soaking, the beef:

1 Tbsp. cold water
1 Tbsp. soy sauce
½ Tbsp. cornstarch
1 Tbsp. cooking oil to be added later

½ pound flank steak (about 1 cup), sliced in pieces
   1½ inches long and ¼ inch thick (a sharp knife will
   be needed; do not use without having an adult
   present)

½ pound snow peas
2 slices ginger root
2 stalks scallions cut into 2-inch pieces
5 Tbsp. cooking oil
¼ Tsp. sugar
1½ Tbsp. soy sauce

Ingredients for Chinese cooking: ginger root, green onions, eggs, shrimp, sauces, and won ton wrappers.

Marinate the beef slices with the soy sauce, water, and cornstarch half an hour before cooking.

Snap off the ends of the snow peas and pull off the strings or fibers from the edges. If peas are large, cut in half. Rinse and drain. (Frozen snow peas may be used.)

Carefully heat 2 Tbsp. of oil in the wok over medium heat and stir-fry the pea pods for about 1 minute, holding the pan with a potholder. (Use extreme caution with hot oil. It may cause serious burns, as well as catching fire itself, if spilled.) Remove the snow peas, leaving the oil in the wok. Add 1 Tbsp. oil to the beef slices and mix. Pour 2 Tbsp. oil into the same wok and heat on high heat for half a minute. Add ginger root and scallion pieces and stir for a moment. Then add the beef slices and stir-fry until they just change color and the pieces are separated. Add the pea pods, soy sauce, and sugar; stir thoroughly. Drain before serving, with an adult helping to hold the pan.

Serve with rice cooked according to directions on the package.

CHINESE AMERICANS TODAY

Although the Chinese have made remarkable progress adjusting to American society, some problems remain today. Their Asian appearance marks them as different from America's white majority, or from African Americans, Hispanics, and American Indians. They are still victims of racism and discrimination.

Education   The Chinese immigrants' drive to excel in education has helped them fit into American life. It has also caused them some problems. Non-Chinese students sometimes resent them for their success in school. The students feel that they have to work harder to compete with Asian students for grades or for admission to colleges. At the same time, Asian students say that, compared to whites, they do not get a fair number of places in good colleges.

Employment   Chinese Americans still earn less than white Americans. They have been kept out of some high-paying jobs and out of many unions. Even Chinese with college degrees tend to make less money than white workers with similar educational backgrounds. Many Chinese Americans can get good jobs, but they cannot win promotions to managers' jobs. Some employers do not put Chinese in positions where they could hire and fire white workers.

Discrimination   Chinese Americans suffer from a growing wave of anti-Asian prejudice. Asian immigrants have been coming to America at the same time that more and more factory jobs have disappeared. Some workers have been forced to compete with immigrants for jobs. At the same time, Japan and Korea have been very successful in selling automobiles, electronics, and other goods in the United States. Some people believe that this has taken jobs away from American workers, causing resentment against all Asians.

Another problem is that many of the newest Asian immigrants are poor and uneducated. Even Chinese Americans whose families have been here for generations suffer from the prejudices that these immigrants arouse. It is not unusual for a Chinese American to be asked, "Where did you learn to speak such good English?" when his or her family has been in America for more than one hundred years.

> We're still not fully integrated into the mainstream
> because of our yellow skin and almond eyes. Much
> has changed in 100 years (since the Exclusion Act),
> but we still cannot escape the distinction of race.
> —Diane Fong, *New York Times*, May 1, 1982

Not all Chinese Americans fit the image of the "model minority." Some battle poverty in Chinatowns faced with the same problems that plague many urban areas.

Chinese students raised a "Statue to Democracy" during their protests for freedom in Beijing in May 1989.

THE CHINESE STUDENTS

Events in China are still causing Chinese immigrants to come to the United States. In June of 1989, a large group of Chinese students staged a demonstration on Tiananmen Square in Peking. They were demanding freedom and democracy for the people of Communist China. Many of these students had studied in the United States. That is where they learned about democracy. The Chinese government broke up the demonstration by killing several hundred of the students.

Most Americans were outraged by the killings and were very sympathetic to the students. At the time, about 40,000 Chinese students were in the United States studying at hundreds of universities. Nearly all of them supported the students in Peking. After the massacre, they were afraid to go back home. They feared that their government would imprison them. The U.S. government has let them stay. Like the stranded students of the 1950s, many of these students will probably become citizens. They will help build America just as the earlier students had done.

AMERICAN IMAGES

On Chinese New Year you may see colorful dragons writhing and bobbing through a suburban shopping mall. Fireworks light up the sky over Chinatowns in New York and San Francisco. Children laugh and giggle as they try to eat fried rice with chopsticks. Beautiful jade carvings and silken robes decorate shop windows. These are now familiar images in America. America is much richer for having included the Chinese in its mosaic of immigrants.

A festive dragon dazzles onlookers during a Chinese American New Year parade in New York City.